THE EARLY YEARS

Gene Simmons and Paul Stanley

Photography by Waring Abbott

THREE RIVERS PRESS

NEW YORK

Published by Three Rivers Press, New York, New York.
Member of the Crown Publishing Group,
a division of Random House, Inc.

www.randomhouse.com

Three Rivers Press and the Tugboat design are
registered trademarks of Random House, Inc.

Printed in the United States of America

Design by Harold Smith with Dan Demetriad/
Demetriad Creative Media, Inc.

Library of Congress Cataloging-in-Publication-Data
is available upon request.

ISBN 0-609-81028-6

10 9 8 7 6 5 4 3 2 1

First Edition

Acknowledgments

Thanks to Laura G. and Ken "The Whip"
Antonelli of Red Distribution—without their
encouragement this never would
have happened.

After that, the work was done by my
editor Kristin Kiser, with Claudia Gabel
and Leta Evanthes. They were very patient.

Also Bill Randolph, Jay Myrow, and Julia Lord
(who still wears some of my wife's clothes).

In the beginning there was
Carol Ross, who helped make a lot of
these photos happen.

And most important of all, Harold Smith,
my spiritual advisors Larry and Curtis,
and Dr. Sara Denning.

Introduction

March 23, 1974, was the first time I photographed KISS and it was an evening that I can still remember 28 years later. As a music photographer, you wind up shooting thousands of bands, but only a few stand out. This was one of them. This is still one of them...

The band had just started out and was opening for Argent, a "progressive" U.K. group. Very soon Argent would be opening and KISS would be headlining.

The concert was at Howard Stein's Academy of Music on West 14th St. in NYC. Later on, the "Academy" would become a trendy disco and then finally a dormitory for New York University. But in 1974, Stein was producing concerts there almost every night of the week, and it was the place to be, particularly for struggling writers and photographers—there was a green room loaded with drinks and food for the press. I would eat as much as I could hold and then fill my camera bag with enough to last me until the next concert. Wherever you are, thank you, Howard!

I had been assigned by a German pop magazine to get live shots of Argent; there had been no mention of any other band. Nevertheless, it was always a good idea to use up a few rolls of film on the opening acts. After all, they might amount to something someday...

The Academy had a wonderful photo pit that allowed photographers to move freely in front of the bands without getting in the way of the audience. When this strange-looking group (all leather was not the norm in 1974) came on stage, I instinctively moved in front of Gene. Any guy with a giant skull and crossbones on his chest must have something going on, I thought.

That was a mistake. He suddenly belched a giant burst of flame directly over my head. I should have taken that as a warning. Fifteen minutes later, my cameras and I were covered in "blood." I wiped it off and kept on shooting. This band was so far out, but they had to be going places, and I wanted to go with them.

When I turned around in the pit, there was a whole row of young women jammed up against the barricade. These girls were screaming, waving everything they had and going absolutely out of their minds. I wasn't used to this kind of reaction. In the '70s, people did not often get hysterical at concerts. Young, excited women were a reliable barometer of success.

But it wasn't all just fire, blood, and deranged fans. The music was loud, nasty, in-your-face rock 'n' roll. And if you didn't like it, they didn't care. It was an attitude that struck a chord with many of us, both then and now.

I wound up working with KISS and did many more stories on them for German and Japanese magazines. What you will see here are the results of those assignments—some of the best-known pictures and some that have never been seen before. No one asked to take anything out, no one made me put anything in. What you see is what I thought would tell the real story of "The Early Years."

It was a wonderful thing to reconnect with Paul and Gene and get their point of view on the pictures and what was going on. We were usually so busy doing these shots, we never had a chance to stop and talk about them.

Thanks to all those KISS fanatics who made this possible, and thanks to Gene, Paul, Ace, Peter, and Eric for taking me along...

Waring Abbott

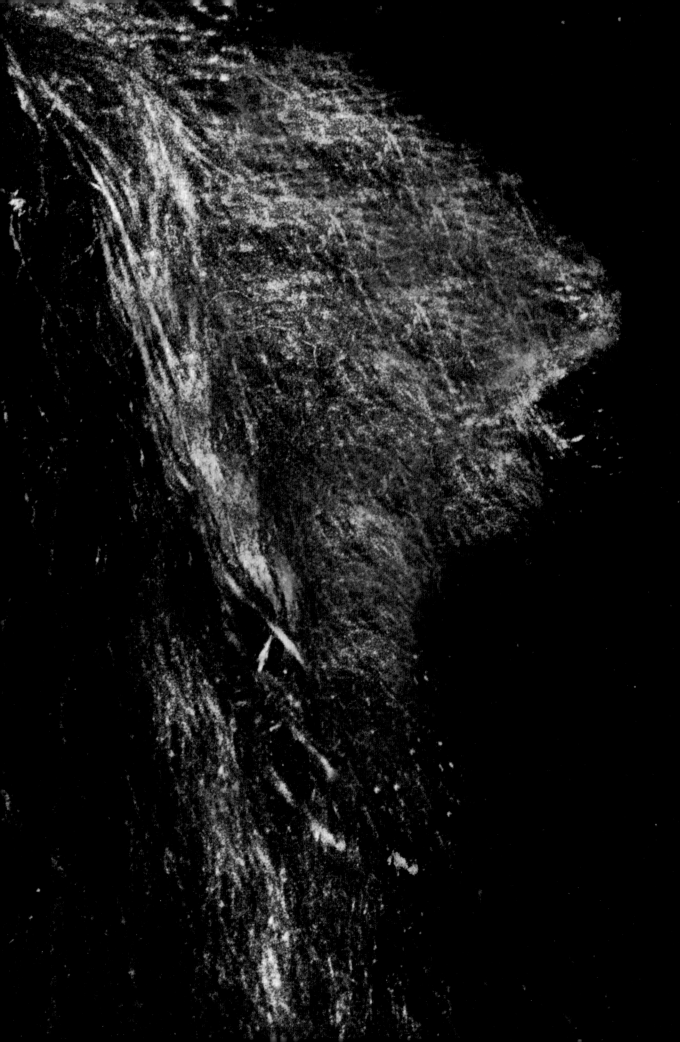

chapter 1   live in ny/nj   1974

PAUL I remember these early shows so well because there was a great buzz about us, which made it all the more important to fulfill people's expectations each time we stepped out on stage. You will see the KISS logo on the side of the stage in some of these shots. At this particular show, we couldn't fly it behind us. We made it a rule that there would be no show without the logo. We not only wanted to leave ears ringing and brains numb. We also wanted to burn our name into people's retinas. It was literally a matter of life or death for the band when we stepped on stage in those early days. My attitude about every show was that we weren't going to get a second chance, so I was going to seize the moment.

GENE We had barely finished recording our first album, *KISS*, which had failed to tear up the charts, yet we were making a big impact on stage, stealing the spotlight from headliners like Savoy Brown and Manfred Mann, and then from Argent, Foghat, Golden Earring, New York Dolls, ZZ Top, and Black Sabbath. We kept opening up for group after group, but it wouldn't last long. None of these bands wanted us to open the show, because we would literally blow up the stage and leave it a mess. In fact, once we opened for Black Oak Arkansas in Charlotte, North Carolina, and within fifteen minutes, by the time we'd performed "Firehouse," I had spit fire from my mouth and the Black Oak Arkansas stage curtain caught on fire, ruining their set.

GENE During the *Hotter Than Hell* KISS era, we played from five to seven shows a week. We spent the days sleeping in the back of a station wagon, driving as much as 300 miles a day, trying to catch extra sleep and get to the show on time. Our road crew would drive through the night with costumes made of leather that would be sitting in wardrobe cases that didn't have any

air ducts. At the very least, the costumes would stink. Often, in cold weather, especially in winter, my costume would become stiff as a board. You could literally stand my costume up in the corner. In order for it to become pliable, the wardrobe mistress had to put it on top of the radiator, so it would warm up. This back and forth from hot to cold, from solid to pliable, not only made the costume stink more, it eventually tore down the leather, so I had to get another outfit made. But all of it—the stink, the discomfort, and the weariness of traveling—helped me get much more into my demon persona.

PAUL I remember early on, through the black leather and studs, that we all had the problem of not being able to move as easily as we wanted and also of not having dry clothes to wear from show to show, as they would still be soaking wet. It was at that point that I started wearing spandex. While at first those in the band scratched their heads, it wasn't too long before everybody was wearing it.

GENE We had our show, we had our levitating platform, we had our bombs, we had our costumes, and we had our KISS logo. We refused to play anywhere that didn't allow us to put up our show, no matter who we were opening up for and no matter how short our onstage performance. Some of the concert halls simply weren't big enough to hang the KISS logo above our heads. So here we are at Lafayette's Music Center in Pennsylvania with our lighted KISS sign sitting on stage. The show was always too big for the halls. Either the pyro put too much smoke in the air, or the drum riser couldn't levitate because the stage couldn't hold the weight, or the seating was too low. Either way, KISS would always go on. KISS would always perform on time, period, and would always deliver the goods.

PAUL Having grown up admiring all the guitar heroes of the day, I was bent on being so much more than just another guy playing chords. Like many others, I spent untold hours in front of a mirror before I could play, making sure that once I could, I would look cool. In the beginning when it came time to decide who was going to speak on stage, it was clear very quickly that no one in the band understood the importance of creating an atmosphere and a connection to the audience that turns the act of being the spokesman on stage into a performance unto itself. From the smallest clubs to the largest stadiums in the world, I've always envisioned myself as being more like an evangelical preacher leading a congregation in praising rock 'n' roll than simply some guy introducing a song list.

GENE We were all trying to figure out who we were and what KISS meant. Early on in the club days, everybody tried to talk on stage. Peter, in particular, when we played the Daisy on Long Island, would take over the mic and say hello to his friends, who had come to see him from Brooklyn. But we soon agreed that Paul should be the voice of KISS instead. Peter's thick Brooklyn accent couldn't be understood, certainly not in middle America. And there was this big notion that something was wrong about the drummer talking between the songs. Ace, although very lovable, had a high-pitched voice and a Bronx accent, and you never quite knew what kind of mood he was going to be in, so that didn't really work, either. When I speak, I tend to sound too much like a school-teacher, which would have certainly diluted my blood-spitting, fire-breathing demon image. That left Paul, with his stage Southern accent. He was and continues to be the voice of KISS.

PAUL Part of what made Gene so powerful to an audience, particularly in the beginning, was that there was no reference point in terms of who he was, where he came from, or what he was truly like. It was that unknown quality and no one knew who existed behind the makeup. It was truly Nosferatu in the flesh. There was an insanity and a commitment to what Gene came to embody on stage that is undeniable when you see photos like these. I believe it was during this time that he was in his purest form and at his very best.

GENE We never really had a chance to practice long enough. After we recorded the songs that comprised the album *Hotter Than Hell,* we went directly back out on tour. I can remember making more than my fair share of mistakes on bass. Sometimes I'd keep the bass neck very high up and make believe I was really getting into it, but, in fact, I was looking at my fret board, because half the time I couldn't remember how the bass figure went. At other times, when I was fairly confident of what was going on musically, I lowered the bass neck and took my "rock 'n' roll" stance. Truth is, though, that once I became the demon, it would envelop me. My heart would pound, adrenaline would run through my system, and I would lose myself. My story in KISS is very much a Jekyll and Hyde fable with guitars.

PAUL There was no book on how to be KISS or how to become KISS, so it was always a learning experience where need led to an answer. Did KISS wear make-up? Yes, of course. Then the question becomes: Where do we put it on? It was easy at a club or a concert venue, but to do photo sessions, particularly in the beginning, we needed the proper space and lighting to make the transformation. It was the start of what was to become the tradition of the band. It's interesting to see the makeup in these photos as we were still learning how to apply it. No one ever taught us, so it was purely trial and error. Sometimes it meant going on stage and being blinded by makeup running into our eyes or spitting it out while we sang.

GENE Early on, I would sometimes not realize that I had kept my T-shirt on and so I'd get fully made up, tease my hair and spray it, and then remember that I had to take my T-shirt off. That, of course, messed up the makeup, which meant I had to apply it all over again.

GENE The process I used to put on my makeup first involved completely covering my face in Stein's Clown White. Then, with a pencil, I would draw my "bat" makeup design on my face, including the widow's peak. Then taking cotton swabs and removing the Clown White from the inside of the "bat" insignia, I would take Stein's Clown Black and fill in the inside of the bat make-up design and the widow's peak, and finally do my lips, too. These were still the early days before any of us learned to put talcum powder or baby powder over the makeup so it would stay on for the duration of the show. The makeup would run very fast. On the other hand, we were usually only on stage for half an hour.

PAUL Ace was, is, and always will be a unique individual. In the early days, he was one of the skinniest people I'd ever met. He was another perfect ingredient for the witches' brew that was KISS. In this picture, Ace is wearing a T-shirt from a club in Nashville we played, called Muther's.

GENE *(NEXT PAGE)* Peter had stopped being Peter Crisscoula only a year earlier. He had come from a very tough street background. Underneath it all was a guy to whom I related, ironically enough, more than I did to Ace or Paul. Peter was in touch with the little kid inside of him and so was I. After the concerts, we would sneak around to each other's rooms to see what kind of goodies we had. We both loved Oreos, Ding Dongs, Devil Dogs, and Hostess cupcakes. Like King Midas taking all his gold and spreading it out in front of him, Peter and I would spread out all the sweets in front of us on a bed and then we'd divide up the goodies.

PAUL For the longest time, people would tell me that I had the thickest hair that they had ever seen. I didn't really know what that meant, because it was on my head. I do remember drying my hair with a hair dryer and never being able to get the roots dry. It was just impossible to dry completely. As time went on, my challenge became: How big and how high can I get my black mane? It was always the cheapest hair sprays that did the trick. I would buy my favorite product of the moment by the case and go through it at an astounding speed. I should've bought those companies or, at the very least, owned stock in them.

It seemed as natural back then as it does today to wear the war paint. That's why whether in full KISS gear or wearing a pair of jeans and boots, my attitude has always stayed the same. Early on, I remember remarks about my chest, that it clearly turned on a certain segment of the female audience. Never having been known for subtlety, I followed the old adage: When you've got it, flaunt it.

GENE We had decided to take a walk through Central Park in New York City on a summer day. What KISS and a park have in common, I'm not sure. What KISS and daylight have in common, I'm not sure, but there we were. Once we were together, however, we knew we had to be KISS, day or night. Ace was spacy, Paul pouted, Peter looked as if he belonged in a street gang, and I looked like as if I had crawled out from under a rock. We were KISS.

PAUL In 1974, we were basically prepping for the onslaught to come. We weren't yet on a tour and we were laying the groundwork for our siege. If a picture's worth a thousand words, we were trying to fill a dictionary. With our visuals being our calling card at that point, it was important to get as much media coverage as we could, and it was important to get as many photos as possible to feed the news media and magazines. At this point, very few knew what was already clear to us: We were on the verge of taking the world by storm.

GENE Here we are in front of the Ziegfeld Theatre, picking a spot to pose for the camera. The two gentlemen on the right could not have cared less; they had to go somewhere and we were simply in the way. But again, we were always KISS; you could tell by our "vibe." We weren't concerned by anything that was going on around us, either. We were KISS, unabashedly and unapologetically proud of who we were.

GENE KISS had yet to become a household name, at least with the masses. So when we walked down the streets of New York, it was to get a rise out of people. But this was New York City. People took everything very matter-of-factly there, even in 1974.

PAUL Having been a cab driver just a short time before, it was interesting to walk the streets in white face, tights, and eight-inch heels. Months before, I'd been in a yellow Dodge, hoping to pick up a fare to Kennedy Airport. Welcome to rock 'n' roll.

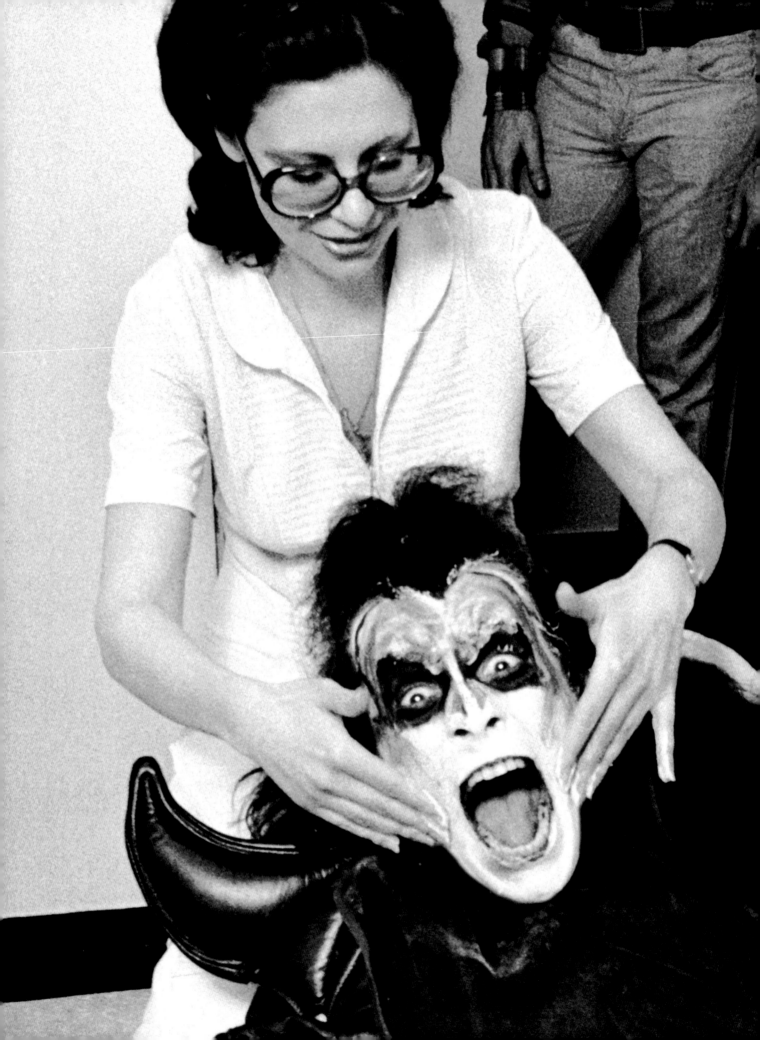

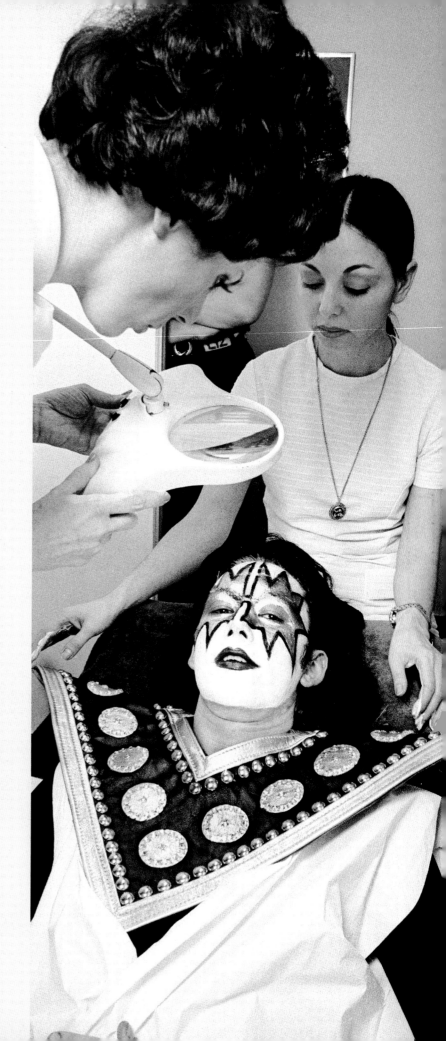

GENE We had gone to a famous beauty salon to get facials. *People* magazine had become aware of KISS and was about to do an article on the band. Our debut in a national magazine. I'm sure the idea was: Those KISS guys wear all that makeup and, well, it must wreak complete havoc on their pores. So, of course, they have to go to a beauty salon to get their pores cleaned, right? Wrong. Nothing could've been further from the truth. We never thought about beauty salons, much less about going to them.

PAUL This was one of those bizarre instances where we were doing anything to get media coverage. Georgette Klinger's, one of the premier high-echelon facial salons, had us come in for what I'm sure they thought would be beneficial media coverage for them also. The fact that they were there to give us facials and we were there to ham for the camera didn't exactly accomplish what the Klinger people had in mind.

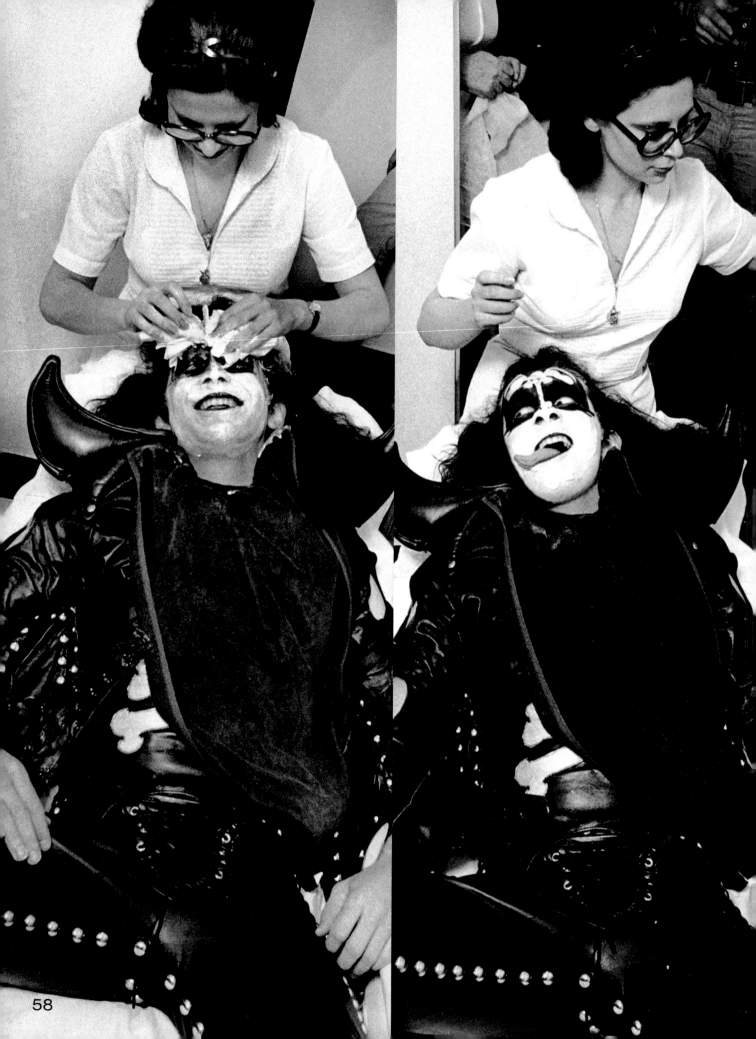

GENE

If I saw an opportunity to mug for the camera, I would take it. I wasn't sure I knew what they had in mind, but I imagined that they thought I was going to sit there quietly while some beautician took a look at my pores. I, however, saw the chair as a torture chamber. When I first started making faces, looking as if I was being tortured, the beautician looked a little perplexed, but soon broke into fits of laughter as she joined in the fun. Of course, most of the time I was looking at the press or the other beautician on the other side of the camera.

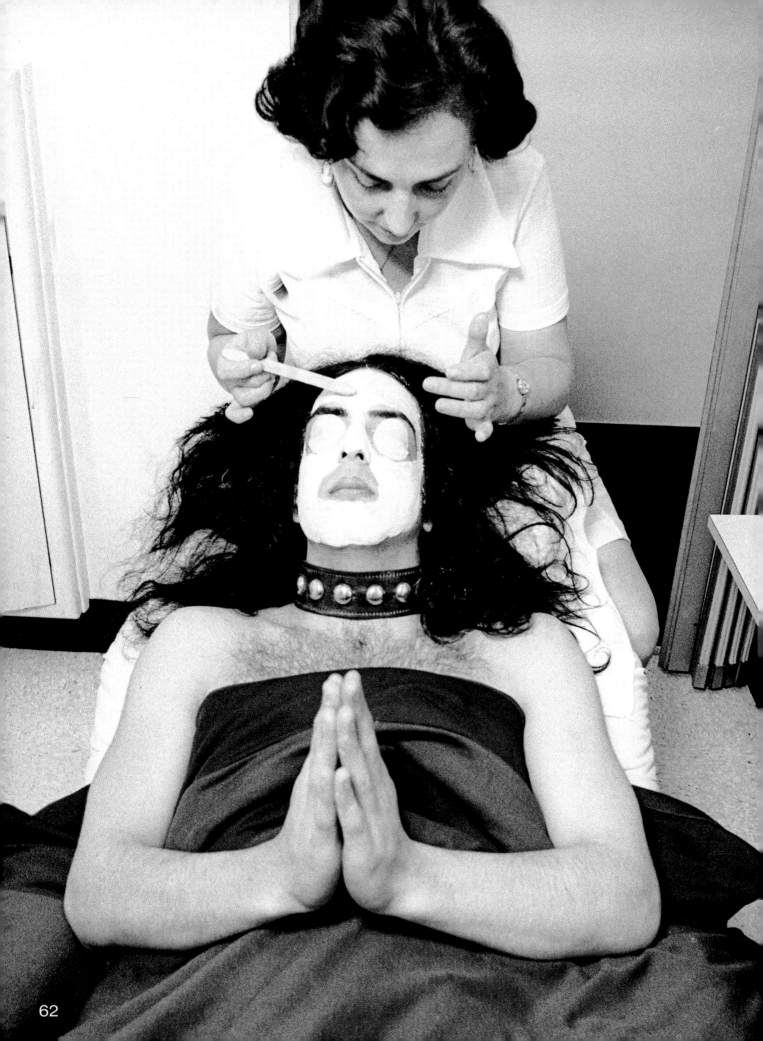

PAUL The Klinger facial episode was one of those events that early in our career seemed necessary and that later in our career would have been out of the question. Still, one has to realize that as bizarre as it is to look at the photos now, it was infinitely more bizarre to have been the subject of them.

PAUL We had heard about a high school football team in Cadillac, Michigan, that suddenly found itself in first place after a long losing streak. The team said it won the state championship, in part, because members listened to KISS music before each game. They said they wanted to thank us personally for our role in their success. Rock 'n' roll has always attracted outcasts, black sheep, and bad boys, so the idea of being invited to a city in middle America to attend a parade thrown in our honor was surreal, to say the least.

GENE In 1975, we were still at the beginning stages of the KISS tsunami, but it was obviously still gathering force and momentum. We had just headlined our first Cobo Hall concert appearance in Detroit to a sold-out audience of 10,000 people. We stopped in Cadillac on our way to playing a show in Flint. It was one of our rare days off, and we were dog-tired. Little did we know that what was awaiting us there would soon blow us all away.

PAUL We were invited to Cadillac for a victory celebration, but I never expected the scene to be such a spectacle. We were greeted as heroes, and everyone was wearing KISS makeup...from little children to school faculty—even the mayor. It all pushed the boundaries of reality.

PAUL Cadillac had become KISS World. The innocence and wonderment of the younger kids was really something to see. I'm not sure most of them understood what the excitement was all about. For them, it probably seemed like an extra day of Halloween.

GENE When we arrived in this small town, it was clear that KISS mania had pervaded the entire community. We saw parents and their kids, state and local political figures and their wives, all in KISS makeup. Oddly enough, everyone felt comfortable with one another—them with us, us with them—despite how unusual this situation was.

GENE When we got to Cadillac High School, our photographer, Waring Abbott, suggested we run out on the football field and fool around. We were trying to emulate that scene in *A Hard Day's Night*, where the Beatles are clowning around on a soccer field. As much as we tried to imitate the Beatles then, we eventually realized KISS had its own unique magic that could never be duplicated.

WARING This was a dream come true for a photographer. Everywhere you turned, there was one great shot after another. Four larger-than-life creatures set down in small-town America, the kind of town I came from. Everyone was excited, everyone was happy.

WARING Doing photos of Paul could never be called work. With most famous people, you had to persuade them to take chances and try something different. Not so with Paul. He was always willing to try something new and he never got tired of being on the other side of the lens.

PAUL Am I a ham? No, I'm the whole pig. The secret to a good picture is a good prop. It's hard to think of a greater contrast than KISS and trombones, which is why these photos are still so amusing.

WARING Even though I had been the drum major of my high school band and then a music major in college, nothing prepared me for this surreal parade up and down the football field. No one asked the guys to pick up band instruments. They just did, and off they went. As usual, their photo ideas were way ahead of mine. I shot and changed film as fast as I could, but I still missed some great pictures.

GENE The football team had even gone and named plays after KISS songs like "Deuce" and "Strutter." That way, the coach and the team knew exactly what those secret phrases meant and no one else would. It was as if we were part of another type of underground society. Whether we were tossing the football around with the team or joining the Cadillac High School marching band, I couldn't shake the feeling that something was about to happen to us— something big. This whole experience was wonderfully bizarre.

PAUL As strange as all of this may look—the band huddled up with the entire

Cadillac High School football team—there was an incredible sense of pride in knowing

that no other band, even in its wildest dreams, could inspire people the way KISS did.

GENE Usually, I'm the biggest guy in the crowd. But somehow one of the bigger linebackers managed to pick me up off the ground as if I were a small child. It was just one of the many extraordinary things that happened during our brief stay in Cadillac, Michigan.

PAUL Even the cheerleaders (pages 94 and 95) were showing their KISS spirit. It's strange to think that just a few years earlier KISS had been nothing more than a dream, and now here was an entire town infected by the virus we had become.

PAUL For a band quickly becoming rock royalty, it was strange to be playing a "private" concert at a school for a few hundred people. But then again, what has always made KISS exciting for me has been the situations we've found ourselves thrown into. With few exceptions, our mantra has always been: We'll try anything once.

GENE The students lost their inhibitions very quickly and forgot that they were in a school auditorium. Before long, it was like a legitimate KISS concert. They were all over one another, trying to rush the stage.

PAUL After our antics on the field, we waved a final goodbye and a helicopter descended to pick us up. As we lifted off, we realized the doors wouldn't close. With each of us using one hand to hold on for dear life, we threw leaflets proclaiming "KISS Loves You" to the thousands below. What a day.

PAUL Here we are in Terre Haute, Indiana, where the city's nonbelievers were converted. It took an army of dedicated rock 'n' roll fans to show a local radio station that, like a restaurant, it is their obligation to serve up what the customers want—in this case, a large helping of KISS.

GENE As the story goes, thousands of fans surrounded the radio station there, and the newspapers reported that, indeed, the "KISS Army" had encircled the building, demanding that KISS be heard on the airwaves. Thereafter, the "KISS Army" became synonymous with KISS fans around the world, and they have been loyal to us ever since.

PAUL Everything had a dreamlike quality to it in 1975 because we were starting to see what we had hoped for become reality. Everyone wanted to be a part of the KISS phenomenon. I've always said that you may not be able to look like KISS, but you can always feel like KISS.

PAUL When in doubt, show skin! I had reached a point where I realized that a hairy chest, to most females, was hot. Notice Paul McCartney looking over my shoulder. In the words of the Who: "Meet the new boss / Same as the old boss."

GENE Being in KISS was very infectious, not just for Peter, Ace, Paul, and myself, but also for journalists who, having never heard of us, soon became enchanted by the magic of the band. Here, Peter was cozying up to a writer who was hired simply to conduct an interview, but who later ended up following us to a number of cities and becoming a new inductee into the "KISS Army."

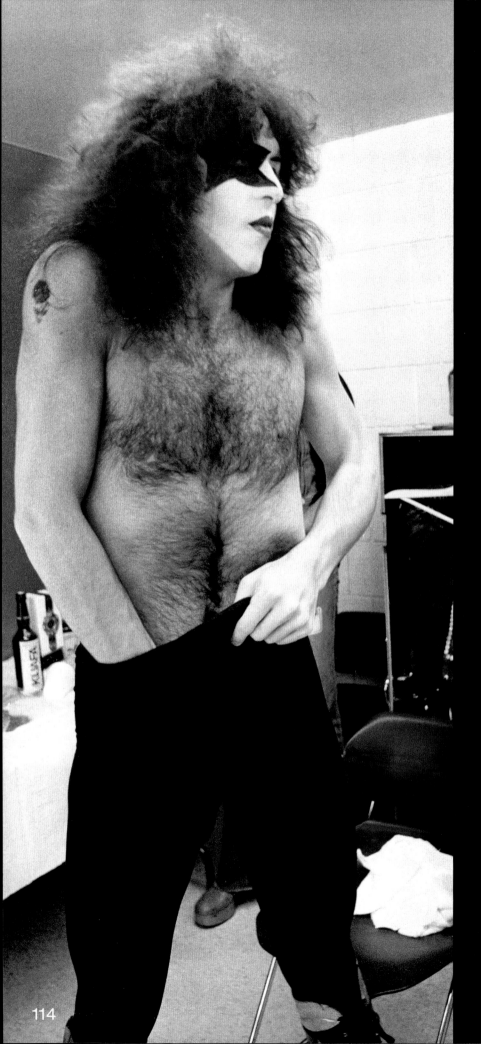

PAUL Since suiting up for a show involved a lot of preparation, it always felt to me as if I were a boxer locking himself into his dressing room to get ready mentally and physically for battle. Although I was a big fan of many of the bands we played with, I believed that the friendship ended when we hit the stage: only one band should be left standing.

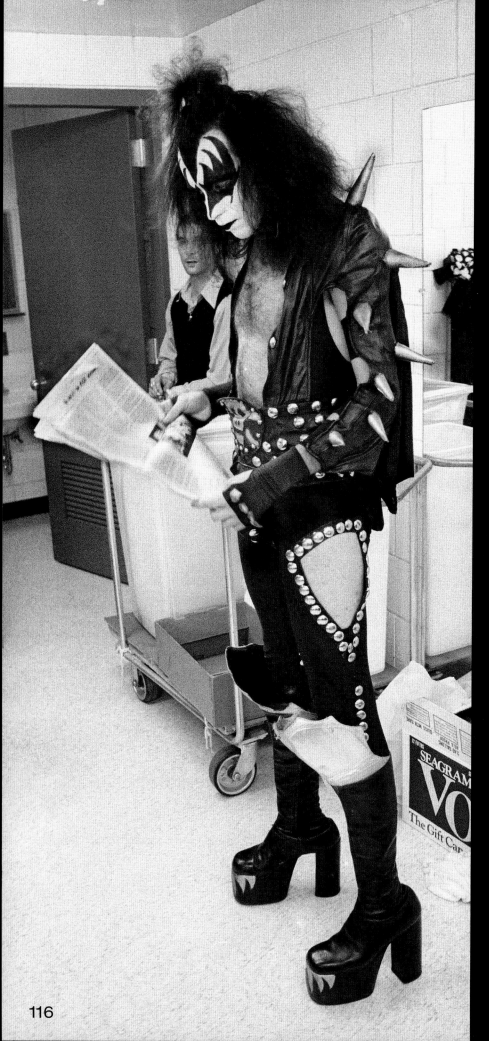

GENE No, that's not the *New York Times*. It's actually the Cadillac High School newspaper. Someone handed it to me right before a show. It was a hoot to glance at the blow-by-blow descriptions of our unbelievable visit there.

116

GENE There was a very real camaraderie in the band, and we certainly had an "us against the world" mentality. The Ace, Paul, Peter, and Gene Team. Anyone who messed with one of us would have to deal with all of us. Everybody worked hard and played well. Those were very innocent times.

PAUL For everything you gain, you give up something else. In order to play stadiums, we had to sacrifice having physical contact with our fans. There is no substitute for being in front of a sea of outstretched hands. The downside of that was performance nights like one at the Tower Theatre in Philadephia, where I found my butt bare and my tights pulled down to half-mast. Still, contact with the audience is what I have always believed is essential to a live rock 'n' roll performance. I didn't get into this business to build a wall between myself and the people who put me here.

PAUL Very few things can compare to getting off the KISS jet and being met by throngs of loyal followers. Sometimes it would be so cold outside that someone would have to cover us in robes to keep us warm. How could we not meet people who were willing to wait outside for hours and freeze their butts off just to catch a glimpse of us? The devotion of our fans has always been amazing and humbling.

GENE Wherever we landed, fans came out in droves to welcome us, even on days like this when the freezing cold weather would have kept any sane person indoors. The young girls were always the most enthusiastic—wanting to hold, touch, and kiss us. Practically everyone was wearing KISS makeup and had soon forgotten that the temperature was below zero.

PAUL Any time a camera was present, the challenge was to turn it into an opportunity for a great photo. What is a guy in eight-inch heels and tights and wearing white makeup doing in a bathtub? Who knows? But it looks cool. Mission accomplished.

GENE In those days, there was never enough time to do photo sessions properly. Actually, there was never enough time to do anything properly. So often, we'd take photos right before a concert was going to start, simply because we were already in costume. For a backdrop, we'd use whatever was handy. In this case, it was the bathroom countertop.

WARING   Gene loved to do "sequences" and so did I. He thought them up in about two seconds and I did the rest. Few magazines would ever run them the way we intended. They would usually print just one shot. Here you finally get to see many of them in sequence, as intended.

PAUL It's amazing how far we've come since those early days. The workload was so much greater, as our preparation for the show not only meant suiting up and putting on our war paint, but also attending to our own instruments. Thankful as I am for where we are today, there's a part of me that misses sitting on that chair and tuning my guitar before the imminent sonic onslaught.

GENE   Before a concert, Ace would spend hours in a room, alone, play-

ing and tuning his guitar. He took pride in his talent as a musician. Ace and I were

very different people who usually went our separate ways backstage, but in front

of an audience, the four of us who were KISS always came together as one.

PAUL Since we kept a rather tight schedule, from time to time we'd have a physician or a venue doctor at our shows. Occasionally, antibiotics might be prescribed if one of us got sick, but mostly the doctors were there just to see how we were holding up in general. Even at our worst, though, the wheelchairs would've been left at home.

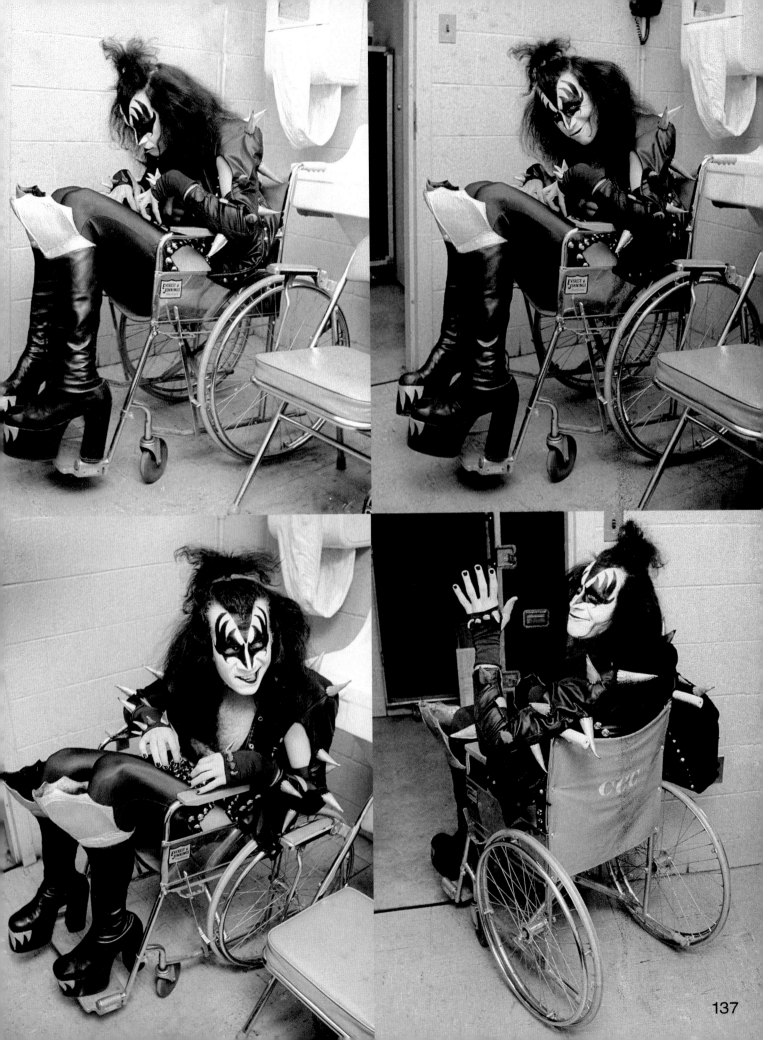

GENE

We would get pep talks from our road managers before shows, very much in the way a football team would. The rest of the guys sometimes let girlfriends tag along. I, however, preferred to be unattached.

PAUL At this point in our careers, we were like kids let loose in a candy store, and our female partners knew it. They tended to insist on coming to cities where they knew, either by rumor or deduction, that we were immersing ourselves, literally, in the local talent.

PAUL Rock 'n' roll is, and should always be, about attitude and flash. Did anyone ever wonder about the deep meaning of Elvis's gold lamé suit? Hell no. I can say definitively and without reservation that nothing could touch us when we were performing on stage. I'm not suspended by wires in the photo showing me up in the air. I could, and still can, jump over your head and part your hair with my boot.

GENE Not too many people know that Ace actually designed, built, and loaded his own guitar effect. His guitar would sometimes start smoking as if it were on fire. Eventually, he would point it upward and a rocket would fly out of it. Ace literally put a stink bomb into one of his pickups and attached a button to the back of his guitar, so that at the right time during his solo, he was able to press it and the guitar would start smoking.

GENE

Meeting and greeting the fans was always important. They were our bosses, they made us who we were, and we owed them everything. We made a concerted effort to spend as much time as possible with our fans and try to give something back to them because they had given us so much. They loved us, and we sure as hell loved them.

WARING Wherever we went, Paul and Gene always took time out to talk to fans and "press the flesh." It made for great pictures, since you never could tell what these guys would do—climbing on top of cars, streetlights, whatever happened to be handy. Gene seemed to be particularly fond of trying to climb chain link fences.

161

PAUL We certainly were about to become something so much more than just a band. For us, it wasn't just about music and merchandise. Our passion for rock 'n' roll and all that it represents was, is, and always will be at the core of our larger-than-life personas.

GENE I had created Frankenstein's monster, which eventually became more important and recognizable than "Gene Simmons." And before I knew it, the fame of my tongue eclipsed everything else about me.

GENE For Ace, being in KISS is what he always dreamed about. I don't think he ever imagined doing anything else.

GENE

By 1981, Peter Criss was no longer in the band and we had welcomed Eric Carr into our family. We had just finished recording *The Elder*, our one and only concept record. All of this marked a period of transformation for KISS. On the outside, our image was different. We cut our hair shorter and changed our outfits a bit. On the inside, we were trying desperately to keep the band together.

PAUL *The Elder* was such a strange period for us because we were trying to move forward and experiment with our music. For many reasons it just didn't work. I don't regret a moment of it, though, because all that I've ever done is a result of what came before, mistakes and all. It took *The Elder* and a few other missteps for us to realize that the best way to move forward is to embrace the past, and in essence who you truly are.

GENE Here we are shooting the video for "I," a song I wrote for *The Elder*. This was all brand-new to Eric, and he played his drums in the video just as dynamically as he would have in a concert hall, even though they weren't amplified and couldn't be heard by anyone on the set. This was exciting for him, and through his eyes we were able to appreciate who and what we were just a little bit more.

GENE Someone had the bright idea to have the fans carry us on their shoulders at the end of the video, but the scene didn't make the final cut. Here, it seems as if everyone in the band was happy, but looks can be deceiving. It was very clear to us that Ace was pulling himself further and further away from KISS. *The Elder* is the only album we'd released that didn't have a tour designed around it. It was also the first album we had released that wasn't successful. We learned a big lesson with that record. We'd hoped to please the critics, but soon realized that the only people we had to please were our fans.

PAUL At the time of *The Elder*, there was a hollowness that was felt by both us and the fans. We were lost but totally committed to continuing forward on our journey. It would be some time before we would figure out how to read the map.

PAUL Cool guitar, cool outfit, cool attitude—but not quite KISS. Still, what has always made KISS work is that beneath the adornments is a vibe and a vision, which even at its murkiest shines through. It shines through like a blinding laser.

GENE The second video we shot was a song called "A World Without Heroes," a ballad cowritten by Paul, Bob Ezrin, myself, and Lou Reed. The video ended with a close-up of my face, a single tear running down my cheek. Bad idea. Demons don't cry.

arriving at Studio 54 for a live satellite Eurovision telecast for the San Remo Festival. It was being seen by millions of people and included performances by groups from all over the world. KISS was brought on to perform "I." It was the only time we had performed as a trio—because Ace never showed up.

WARING This was in the basement of Studio 54, where I had set up a little studio, surrounded by policemen and executive types. We had quite a bit of time to shoot, since we were waiting for Ace to show up, which never happened. I only had the chance to photograph Eric twice, and this was the last time—and the only time we had a conversation. He was very talented and seemed to be excited to be where he was. It was so unusual to run across someone in the music business who truly loved what he was doing and did it well. He was a great subject

197

PAUL What do you do when the cameras are about to roll and a member of the band is nowhere to be found? You go out and kick ass. The show must go on.

PAUL It's strange to think that *The Elder* period came about because of our own complacency with our fame, our newfound interest in getting approval from our peers, and advice from our inner circle. It was time to "grow" and show everyone what brilliant musicians we were—a sure recipe for disaster. It all starts with loving what you do and pleasing yourself. Without that, you might as well drive your car off a cliff, pedal to the metal.

PAUL Lights, camera, action. Beamed through the miracle of satellite technology to countless millions of homes throughout Europe, we completed the job we set out to do. Three members of KISS are better than four members of most other bands. Crank it up and rock the world.

PAUL It was always good to see the legions of fans who supported us through this shoot. Like any family, we were all in this together—through both the good and the bad.